Down Their Spears

Jared Pearce

Cyberwit.net

HIG 45 Kaushambi Kunj, Klidipuram
Allahabad - 211011 (U.P.) India
http://www.cyberwit.net
Tel: +(91) 9415091004 +(91) (532) 2552257
E-mail: info@cyberwit.net

This book is dedicated to my parents,

Richard and Lorna Pearce.

Special thanks to

Joseph Eakins, who designed the section lines, and

Katie Wheeler, who created the drawings and etchings.

When the stars threw down their spears,
And water'd heaven with their tears,
Did he smile his work to see?
Did he who made the Lamb make thee?

—William Blake

The Poem

I
Scholars' Conventicle at Noph, Temple Discourse

The hour's come
my students, friends,
and colleagues. Abrahm
is my name, and through that
name Pharoh sends

me to you, here,
in this temple to teach
astronomy as learned in Ur
of the Chaldees, and all
the learning of each

star and planet,
and of the creation
as we have recorded it
from our fathers and traditions:
How this planet's one

God opened his eye
onto a flat space, his pupil
a disk that will lie
flat for us from every angle,
from every end a circle:

a plenary illusion,
the mages call that black
hole. For it is the one
thing in the universe not of
universal matter; in fact, it pulls back

to see its matter itself!
This mystery shall be
explored, my friends, for how else
can it be seen, being
the opposite of every

object? From what's not
there, from the absence
of matter. Now what
does this mean — how is this
seen and known? The eye picks up tints

from flowers, from faces;
we live the life of reflected
light, of appearances
floating over reality. But God's eye
has no reflection, has no dead

covering such as other
matter. Yet its traces are seen
in how it pulls on its neighbor
stars — as if matter wanted to get
back to the center where the greatest being

wields a power both above
our normal thoughts and through
them. Here is no mystery trove,
but observable phenomena, a tendency,
as we'll see, for this power is the glue

and the unglue of the universe. This is
the first mystery, my friends,
that the Creator opened His
eye onto space, onto matter,
a yet dark and horrendous

lack of motion. For atoms
were packed tight as scallops—
an infinite density with no crumbs
drifting, sheer pressure without
ignition. Though He knows its stops

He cannot disturb it, cannot have
it dance directly, for to do this a certain
line would be crossed, and His staff
must stay behind or our space would
annihilate from His glory, in

less than a blink, flames
to melt all our isolations. In geometry
and physics is this not the claim:
that if a line of light
is split in a crystal we

observe its parts, but only
by whole white light.
If we could see
through, from a split light a portion
of those split would not ignite,

and so it is here:
an infinite line behind
God's pupil at the center
of the universe, and a matter
so dense, so crystalline

that it had stopped moving,
held back from God's
pupil. And His eye a spring,
a conduit in this matter, opening
between existences that shod

one another, effect each
other, yes. You see? Both
informing, both in reach
yet secret from chaos's dark
names. There was a pure oath

between God and the material
here, that here's the right
place for a world without dull
wasting, if humans can keep
everything in order. You see, this site

then is for ordering, by
order. Hmm, ah, but we're off
track, hmm — where was I?
And Abrahm, seeing the sun
set and the sacrifice to Thoth

burning in the courtyard,
turned to his listeners —
some waiting, others bored
by his tale, or suspicious. He begins
an end: Hmm, every beginning is sure,

a point fixed on a plane. And matter
rested near death, for the Eye
is matter but various and of a higher
material than the Void He
opened in and by

Himself. Ah, perhaps you are
tired? We will continue
with questions and experiments far
into the cosmos. For now
let's adjourn, and I'll meet you

at the observatory in deep
night. Yes, let's rest
and prepare ourselves to peep
into the mighty heavens of God,
His throne at the center best

seen after midnight in this
country. And Abrahm left
his brothers, speaking together: I resist
these ideas, although, at Abrahm's
words I felt bereft

of my own. But, something
we can't observe is provable?
If he can prove it, being
a man of science, I will follow
all his teachings, cull

the deep mines of his
secrets. So will I, but
I really think knowledge of this
type belongs to old women and poets,
folk-tales shut

in his psyche since
the goat-herds started telling
stories; hence,
this nomad relives his youth
and to gain position at court is selling

rehashed ideas and images.
Even if his blatherings are Chaldean
learning, we see how their religious
teachings have infiltrated
their science. A mathematic and pagan

monster with two contrary
heads! — Nothing will
be proved tonight. I disagree,
all learning, especially ancient,
comes from a master with special

insights gained in painful
meditations and journeys.
Let us see what he pulls
from the heavens, what
knowledge and mysteries

he unravels as he picks
up the trace of the unknown
deity. Perhaps his proof will fix
his rambling ideas and physics;
let's find out what he has shown

only glimpses of. And
they met at the observatory
that evening, all their hands
computing distances, their eyes
roving the sky through their glass pottery.

Scholars' Conventicle at Noph, The Eye Opens

You see? my brothers, since
I held that lens and saw, but now
I see a sea,

light and endless, a gripping
land of white forms sharp
as a crocodile's bite

to the eye, and as mighty! In my
mind it roves, eats
entire groves of my brain's loaves:

I am undone as a man — for He will
grow in me — and so how can I stay
the same or say no

to such power? And I saw it,
brothers, the disk, the pupil the hour
it opened and how the sour

land was burnt, there was
glassy ground around Him, and I found

a town of figures whom He asked for
volunteers to zoom down through
doom

and painful glooms to —
Viola! You see? Time starts,

brothers, when Kolob, red
fire leaping off
his sleeves, stepped up, he
said, I will, his hammer gripped

and tripped up into His
mouth and leaves down
past the eave

of His lips — and the tongue
found Kolob, and he felt
he'd been dragged
across the desert stones then
smashed in the teeth,
reduced to a gram with shells
of himself whipping
off as he's stung

with acrid rains
mauling his lid he slid

down the throat of God!
In empty air his feet
seek landing, in that shaft
no craft finds relief
or password to safety, an
infinite reek in the draft

as Kolob loses
direction, orientation,
confuses time and
distance and cruises

crushed in pocket
juices hotter than the maw!
Rocket fuel nibbling
his groins and kidneys,
his lungs and liver
wrenched by the dark
emissions I saw swirl
around his raw

essence now drowning,
lower in God's
eternal bowels:
caverns that lose
the dead howls,
no pause from
the stench and fouls.

And, my brothers, he
did. He is tangled in
leeches and acid
sea weeds wrangled about
his shoulders and
knees; poisonous talons
hook his fetid

eyes, and the ravens
tease him as a man through
a keyhole: twisting his brain
string they pick with
their beaks any leaks
and holes, their wings spring

concrete in between
the recesses and breaks.
A speck, Kolob, his meat
and his freak shoved in
messes of fire! A shower,
my brothers, red heat

gathering him up, you
see: he went down, fallen,
now rises in volcanic
flames and titanic pressure,
he caved in and burnt,
his sizes reduced by degree
and reprises

of pain and pressure
without measure that
comprises a birth out
into new pasture

he's cowed. Ah, splendidly
up and infinitesimally tiny,
a briny concoction towed
faster and faster, he's mowed

and shaved harder and
harder. And as the arterial
wall grows closer and closer he

slows and lines up and his hand
grabs the land

where two meet him,
my brothers, as moths
trim in grey these others
with great brown wings
descend from the shades of
the ceiling: Ariel swings,
Teum glides as if skating.
Hail Kolob, they shout,
From the rim

of God's mind we guard what comes
in; we parcel out any of chaos. You spent
your choice to be the first in His created
space and we honor you. We tell you you
must find the dark cell

and gain entrance. Hail the Name of the Most
High God, who grants passage for these, His
intelligences. Now onward to the entrances
of matter, of space, the frame where we may bring
grace to Him who gave us the same!

Oh, brothers, can
you not see it in this fan
of stars? Behind the palpable
voice making everything
tremble? And Kolob first
dragged himself across
the folds and ridges, then
climbed the cliffs, the infinite
rifts and ledges of His mind.
Gullies lost in depths, he
feels along blind

in the dark holds and
secret tunnels.
But a humming in
his chest like sonar grows
fuzzier as he burrows
and worms in the cold
toward the blank hole.
And brothers, as he's numb
at last and though
delirious he knows

and faints as he topples
the final stones out
the path of the saints,
his finger bones
shattered to dig so
deep to the null disk, yet
he's blown

by a cosmic breeze, he
wakes innocent on a thread
twixt the Abyss and the hiss
and roar of the Void. Brothers,
he drank the lees and alone
he first sees

the bottomless Abyss
of a dream, and his head
spins as he peers out
over its edge without
hedge of a rail. Barely
a seam from this to where
waves of the Void's
annihilation sail
crumbling towards him
from every way then
receding to blossom
and break and scream.

Not knowing where
he was he started
to wander endlessly, you see,
along the faceless
trace of existence,
of space, an infinite
path between fear
of heights and fear
of oblivion. And his orbit
is time, yes, hence the creation
begun and there, you
see that red fire is him,
Kolob, nearest the pit

at the center of the universe,
bowing to God's hidden
throne, yet ridden by hunger
to search for his mate,
the root of his calling,
and all the time lost and made
fat chowing on space!
It was he who first
stirred the matter, saw
the first chutes live; he
began its great ploughing.

2

From Nauvoo, Illinois, 1842

Dear Brother Phelps, Devout in Ministry
to the Lord Most High—
                          I received your note
a day ago, and it awakened me
as barren limbs break into spring: one day
black with sleep, the next buzzing with color.
But don't suppose your meeting George Keats chance,
for God directs all our motions, every last
glance or heart beat. Indeed, if what you say
is true, then if John Keats and I had met
these twelve years since such tales we could have told—
as morning air is clear, so his prophetic
strain's revealed to me: what he called sparks,
intelligences, are our very souls in
making, just as he's intuited.
                                      But
William, hear in closest secrecy, and
I'll reveal to you the Enishgo-ondash,
great governing Ones nearest God's dais
of stars, their holy faces whispering
His name through every core of life—for they're
revealed to Hyrum and I one open night
outside Kirtland before the temple was
raised, the glowing stones under the moon lit
our path between the trees,
                                      we were both caught
up while discussing Abraham's writing
and we beheld the entire creation
of the universe, and we have currently
been revealing portions of this truth to

others initiated amongst us
and prepared, such as yourself.
                                        However,
you must forebear for I cannot tell all—
it takes an eternity to begin
the universe's fate, the revelations
that I've got hot and raw as electric
wire. And since you deem Keats's vision worthy
discussion, his letter speaking beyond
the grave, as it were, to this soul-making
vale, I'll relate some mystery relevant
to the purpose behind this world of tears,
the ratio of dreams and reality
striking through existence like a needle
through cloth; the very stuff Keats's letter both
starts and finishes—but here's the account
straight from God's burning mouth, the marvelous
purposes of material creation,
this mysterious life and its dreamy
revelations; in short, I'll add where Keats
left off silent—and look inside yourself
to know if I'm a prophet:
                                        For Kolob
feared Abyss and Void, wandered endlessly
until one laid before his path, lightning
tipped wings almost extinguished from the long
trial of God's mind: Lucifer, whom
Kolob cured to beat his loneliness by
smoothing down his feathers, curling
Lucifer round with his own cloak.
                                        And when
restored Lucifer arose and said, Hail
Kolob, first in space, and maker of time;
I am sent bringing light to you in darkness,
I too travailed God's wormy acres and
others soon will follow, for our Father
sent us here to sustain you our brother
and lo, Oliblish is here already,

see her lying yonder — Come, let's bring her
round to feel the space created by our God.

They went and raised up Oliblish, they dried
her robes and dabbed the steaming rivulets
that dripped along her hems. As she revived
she said, Among His children are you blessed,
beginning is yours, Kolob, and we are
here to aid you. Kolob looked on Oliblish,
as if she'd risen from a pool of glass,
and loved her instantly: for she was
wise and powerful and good, the first
reflected image he had seen, beauty's
first creation on the wavering cusp
of life.
            And as the three rejoiced in their
meeting, Jehovah crawled from the eye, covered
with splinters and tree leaves and desert dust,
bearing a satchel he approached Kolob:
Here is my errand, to bring creation
to space and you, Kolob. And I propose
that you plough the fields, and Oliblish reap,
I will sow these seeds, and Lucifer will
light our days and track our progress and make
accounts of these our labors in this space
designed for individuality.
Jehovah's plan seemed wise, and the four gods
covenanted to work and help each other,
and Oliblish married Kolob, for she
delighted in his careworn face and gave
herself to him, and he gave himself to her.

Now in the satchel Jehovah carried
were the very sparks, intelligences,
or as the ancient Egyptian has it,
Aieswhiti, and it is the divine plan
that creation be brought into this realm:
These sparks being the very material
of souls to be planted into infinite

matter of space: for matter, even the
immortal soul of man, is infinite
and neither created nor destroyed but
organized, directed, and refined.
                                      And
Kolob saw that the satchel burned an orange
light, and bulged as the pollywog creatures
swam and squished inside a luminous sort
of jelly. He hesitated to touch
one, to pick up a seed: Jehovah closed
the bag and explained he was not ready,
for the furrows must be ordered and the
planting must begin in earnest.

                                          Thus, it begins,
another beginning one could say:
Lucifer counted off a measure
of the horizon-line, and Kolob smote
a chunk off the Void with his hammer which
shattered as a shell under a stone, yet
retrieved mass enough to craft a shear. And
as Jehovah and Oliblish fanned his forge
and brought cooling waters from the Abyss,
Kolob forged a plough wherewith to prepare
space wherefore to plant the seeds. He harnessed
Jehovah and Lucifer to turn, break
thin slices of the Void into hungry,
nourishing soil outward from the center.
And they all planted the first crop, established
canals leading water from the Abyss
to the fields.
         So the process continued
but each performed their part separately and
united: for Oliblish nourished all
creation and reaped it into space, and
Jehovah assigned these new beings to help
the process:
                     The first of these, named the children
of Kolob and Oliblish, were five sons,

Elkeneh, Karesh, Libnah, Mahmarcknah,
and Shinehah, and also daughters Rukeneh,
Senshu, Mintrah, Sepdet, and Jahoheh:
These ten were the first creations brought forth
independently in their sphere, and hold
the rights to their office and all the keys
and powers, and key words of creation
they obtained from their father, and they are
the next pyramid of genesis, thus
building the universe of our God one
block upon another, as one stone lifts
up another, as a temple rises
into the rising sun: Kolob as set
apex, as corner stones Elkeneh as
south-east stands, Karesh as south-west, Libnah
north-west, Mahmarcknah as north-east, and Shinehah
as center stone in the pyramidal
base, and each corresponding to that priesthood
associated with the stones, Shinehah holding
the place where the baptismal font scoops out
earth for redeeming the dead and the point
where the altar juts into heaven, we lay
thereon our desires and promises
to God and Earth's Kingdom: the conduit
positions between this existence and
God's dimension.
                    And this pyramid is
aligned with the matching feminine, outlined
above, and as the corners matched, so did
the centers, and Shinehah and Jahoheh met
and married, and each man gave himself,
and each woman gave herself.
                              These places,
positions, rights, and responsibilities
had they from the beginning, raising a
mosaic beauty and order in the
universe.
             And Lucifer portioned out
area for all these, and they held lands

and worked lands for to bring forth creation,
and Jehovah organized their lots.
                                                   In
the evenings when they rested Jehovah
sang ballads and told his dreams of their life
beyond this realm, and how they came to be
in space, in corporeality, in
love and responsibility.
                                         Now
it so happened that the track around the
Abyss was filled, evenly portioned and
spread until it became the very finger
print of God, furrows of creation spinning
into space and bearing the eternal mark
of the One Lord of All. Lucifer saw
there was no more room for tracts, and sought council
for new areas, for surely more
creation would desire to create
for themselves.
                             After discussing the matter
Jehovah, his face suspended grey
for a second, advised Kolob to plough
upwards from the horizon into the sky
and downwards below, and doing so
the area increased, and creation,
                                         and this,
Brother William, is the matter of how
we, sparks of God as it were, began to
be formed inside the very sphere we both
shape and that shapes us — full of misery,
yes, and pain, but also joy and friendship,
and not many men know this more than I.

But my discourse grows long, and I've many
things to speak on this matter when the time
is more fulfilled.
                               But for now I look
forward to your next report and return as
the Spirit directs. Preaching the gospel

is our portion of creation: to form
and nourish and replenish to our
brethren that which is lost to them, what they
cannot see; it's been lost to the lost world.

JOSEPH SMITH

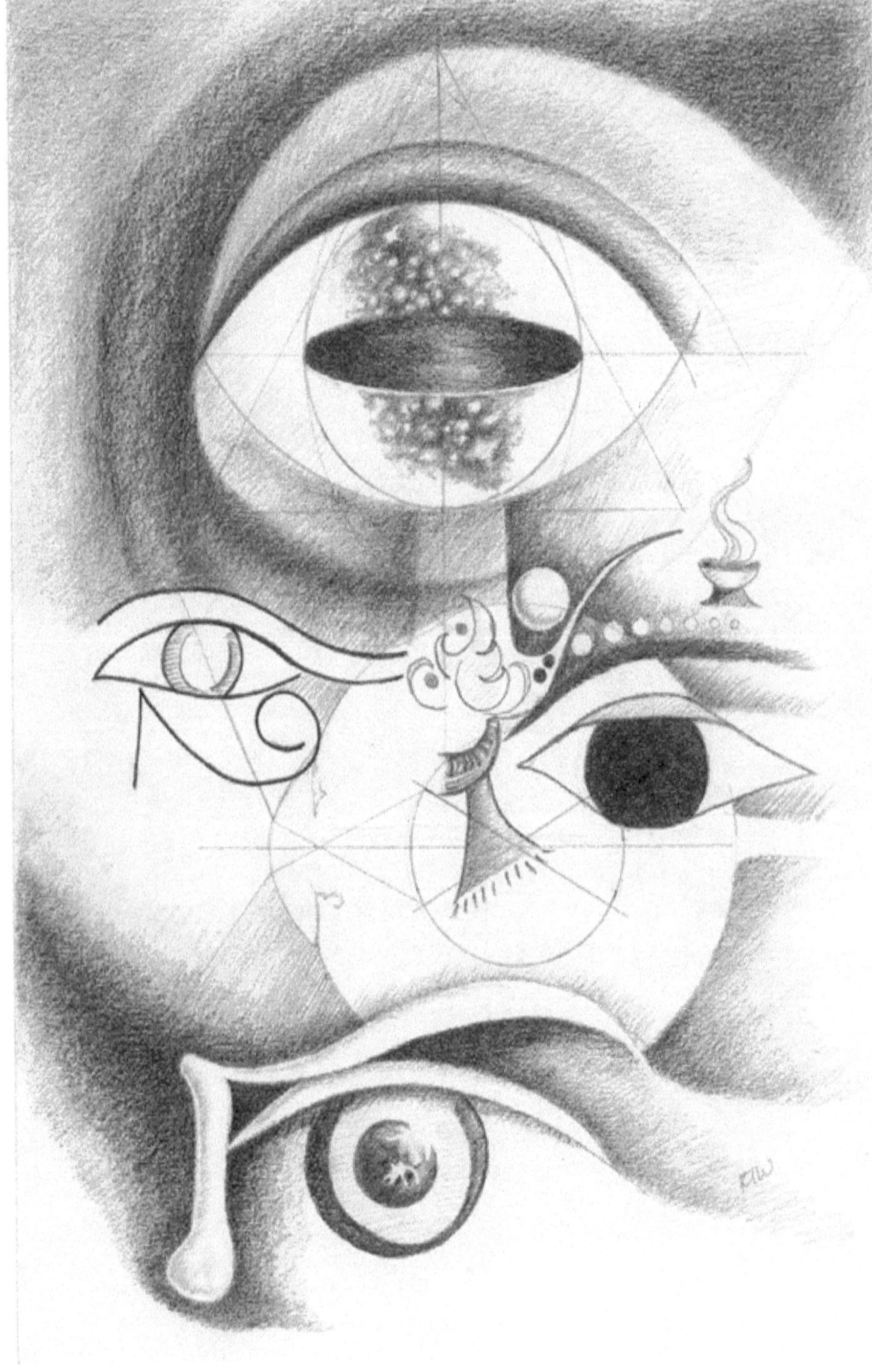

3
From the Prætorium Prison, Constantinople, 836

Oh, it's just like in that vision,
brothers, the one I had of true religion
where Adam, son of noöscopic Shinehah, son of Kolob
near the center of the solar system, like Job
who was thrust in difficulties and despite
mangy bitterness gained light
and grace with God — So let it be with me
and you, Michael the Synkellos, Theophanes,
wherever they've led you both —

for I've come with you here to fulfill an oath
that now seems unfulfillable. It was during our fast
when we wandered from St. Sabas
thirty days into the desert, thirty nights
without water or sleep, scaling heights
in Jesus' desert. And you showed us the stars
Michael, the rising Venus, the descending Mars.

Then we held the vision of Adam's early
days in the first aeon of time, and see
how his position carries ours —
it is our devotion that sours
the covenant; just as Adam followed the crown
of Jehovah earnestly, and in doing so prepared his own
fall: it was he and Eve that brought
forth the tree of Knowledge, it was purity that sought
ignorantly its own destruction.

I seek to breed no corruption
in my thought, but my brother, my father,
recall how Jehovah sought a gardener
through all of space and only Adam and his wife
Eve (being of Marmacknah's earthy clan) had the life
talent to do as requested: bring forth creation
capable of perpetual imagination;
to create beings who would multiply
themselves through space, organize matter and untie
the slow sowing and reaping of agronomic substantiation,
perfect though it was, the system had begun
germination but lacked something
vital, some new speed or efficiency — that's the thing —

Efficiency was the Gods' cry, not just
Jehovah but Lucifer as well — for all the Gods rushed
to and from their lengthening labors: Kolob's plough eroded as it
dragged along space, and the Gods were fed
on their travail yet craved respite.
Are you beginning to see, my friends, the tight
knitting of our lives, our purposes, and aims,
of how we came
into the hungry paw of the fifth lion —
it was justice and mercy led us here, in
our race for piety we have been chosen
sufferers — the painful glory of our choices woven
into our united destinies. Michael,
you pointed out it was with Jehovah's good will
that Adam and Eve constructed a greenhouse
from which to begin their experiments, their vows
made to each other and to the Gods for their work —

Much as we, my brothers, though tortured by the Turk,
have covenanted to bring the Kingdom
to earth, to uphold not just some
of His gospel, but everything from the holy icons
to the supremacy of the Heavenly Father! We are pawns
in the mighty motions of His will,
we spill

how He tips us, and we'll go where He sends
us. And so did Adam and Eve tend
their garden, work in the greenhouse long durations,
each bringing, raising, and naming creations:
Eve found places and names for all
vegetation, and Adam named each animal.

o   o   o

They didn't give me any bandages—
I've strewn straw and dirt along my forehead
to stop the bloody verses branding me a mage
and heretic to the Holy Church; instead
of Astronomer, astrologer, for
Teacher of the Divine Wisdom, mere philosopher.
Yet perhaps there's truth in their pricks and pokes:
I should not have led you here, Theophanes, let the iconoclasts
          and filioques
have their way—is this
true religion? I've sinned only in His
will, in following the Divine Voice, and brother may
you and He have mercy on me. Today
as they finished tattooing our faces
I prayed God this mark will lend me grace:
get beyond the cherubim with flaming sword: for as Paul
          we suffer
for righteousness; our devotional cruciations makes us
          tougher,
may it please God, in the long run.
And now Theophanes, my righteous, perfect muezzin,
though younger more perfect, though gone yet I speak as if
          you were
here; your smiles that I envision in the cell's stone wrinkles
          cure
my loneliness. For as we are
like Adam, obeying though tormented so far
as God permits, so we are like him in that when we grieve
we are not alone—we have each other, he had Eve
to comfort and accompany him in his faithfulness

and sin; if you, my brother in flesh and spirit, were here I'd
          request
a song: Theophanes, you should sing the one Michael wrote—
ah, the tune is an echo of itself, a tease of wind smote
upon a puddle, a whisper in my brain—what was it? I'm
          infandum renovare dolorem,
that hymn—
he wrote, about how Adam first found the tree
of Knowledge? Yes, the story of how he
asked Kolob for one seed, raw, unplanted,
how he brought it home to Eve and enchanted
with the task planted it in a treated soil.
And Jehovah, stopping by, noticed the royal
coloring of the sapling, asked Adam what
sort of tree it was? commented that the leaves put
a tired feeling in the nostril,
and please tell him when it flowered—until—
until I recall the entire scheme I can't close
my eyes: how did it finish?
Ah, yes, no rose
flowered on that tree, no heavy pear
bent its spiny limbs; instead some rare
occurrences grew in regularity: at night, shears
left in the greenhouse would be missing in the morning, tiny
          tears
would be found in papers and charts left near it,
and sometimes a smaller floret
would wilt and die being close to the tree.
Jehovah didn't seem surprised when he
learned it matured cunctatiously; and when the seeds
finally did sprout in indigo weeds
similar to cotton puffs in texture,
they were sterile, despite every fertilizer
Adam and Eve tried; when the tree was placed
at the apex of a genealogy chart it remained chaste
and otiose—the seeds would not grow. Jehovah bade them
          watch it
closely, and aided them as they transplanted it to a patch remote

from the houses, at the far end of the garden, near the compost
        ditch.
              o   o   o

I can barely make out three stars in the niche
of a crack in the wall. Too many days.
I can only pray for you, brothers in Christ Jesus, it has been
        too many days —
How long, oh Lord, shall we endure
the oppressors' mockings, the manacles, the ox-hide torture?
When shall we come to Thee in Thy Holy House,
made without hands, bought without ounce
of money — littered, it is, with Thy Glory just as the Temple
erected by Kolob's sons as a place for assembly, for pupil
and master to corradiate. In the burgeoning beauty
of Adam's garden was it made, I can see
it iridescent through the groves, the Gods coming
and going as they may — and I long to sing
at one of its blessed convocations: take
me, Lord, from this place, shake
the souls of my brothers free from these walls —.

I will fail, Theophanes. I will die here. Our falls
pattern Adam's so nicely. Micro and macrocosm. Neither
did he escape his death. But it is not the body, but aether
that makes me despair: I can never be clean
on this Earth, never breathe in the pure dream
of God, here.
                I can only remember
things I once saw on the mountain, in an ember,
on the desert's scorched plain —
and it is the touch of memory that pains —

the memory of the dream of Heaven,
of cosmic arms gathering me into the celestial den
that so wholly resembles
Kolob's Pyramid, where the hosts assembled
to love, to work, to find the mind of one
the mind of all.

          Through the crack, if I don't breathe, the sun
will rise for I'll see a gold reflection in the slit
but won't actually see it
climb the skies. This is my last lesson: so are we,
brothers, wandering blindly,
stuck in this dungeon which symbolizes Earth under
the blazing of the adorned St. Sophia, the wonder
that all travelers feel when they approach the Byzantine
palace with its thousand chapels is likened to that entering

the very mezzanine of Kolob's Temple, the celestial glory
itself. We will meet again brothers when we are past this gory
existence, meet in Heaven's Pyramid. And I am sorry
being the weakest in faith and body among you, I am sorry
I should be stronger: yet on this Earth I will not see you
          anymore;
I will never see you again, Father Michael, *graptoi* Theophanes,
          my brothers.

THEODORE *GRAPTOS*

4
A Preface from Crotona,
Southern Italy, ~398 B. C. E.

Plato,

     As per our agreement, here is the last chapter —
save one — of the Pythagorean doctrines: *Astronomy*.
Hence, I also notify you I have received, after
our contract, your last payment, and expect your alimony
on its proper date, of forty golden minas; surely
your overstuffed students pay enough tuition that such
sums are minimal to the fat Athenian youth? Thirty
years ago Socrates, some friends and I, over lunch
nearly signed a deal for me to stay with him and his bunch
to philosophize, as he called it. But Master
Pythagoras has a short leash, and I stay in close touch
with any brother who may have survived the disaster
of our leader and our clan which happened much faster
than any of us planned — thus is the wisdom of the race.
But this small story does indeed tie-in to the vaster
tale you requested in your correspondence: at the base
it will inform your writings, and the apex, through disgrace
I admit sections are yet mysterious to me.
                                    Think
of Athena's Harvest Festival, in Athens, the place
where Socrates, Timaeus, and I began to link
Soul to Earth and Earth to Heaven in one eternal rink
of time. Critias and Hermocrates joined the debate,
since they were in town, and learned men. These days with
      the stink
others have made of my Master's teachings, it would mean
      your fate

listing me with erudite company; to date
every single one of my followers has been killed —
you're the sole listener of the only speaker who escaped
the holocaust —
                        At the fête we five sat in discourse, grilled
meat for the others, grapes for me, and our topic tilled
an interesting question: in the history of time
was there one main event besides creation that filled
the universe and led to its infinite expanse? I'm
the one who spilled the beans: the Master's greatest rhyme
dealt with the events of the creation and fall,
and I recited to them the mystery clear as a chime;
clear as five blacksmith hammers in correct proportion all
strike united, so we spoke together on Athens's mall:

And now you ask the same. Strange that Socrates won't speak
in my place. Or perhaps you desire other tangible
sources to correct him? When you see that grubbing old Greek
remind him he owes me for some scrolls — pique
his memory a bit, he'll know which ones I mean. For you I preface
the *Astronomy* with a glimmer, a peek
at Pythagorean wisdom in canto shards, haiku
splinters speaking of difficulty, unity, of how through
this unity there will once again be the harmony
of the celestial spheres.
                        For creation felt a doom
bearing down on it, and even Jehovah dreamt only
of catastrophe: of a pair of lips gold as honey
leaping from dead ashes and spewing forth a rock burning blue
and green, hissing and sizzling and dripping bits of scree.
And the molten ball, despite losing itself, larger grew
and its heat grew until it filled Jehovah's view
and he could only sit at its base and eat one peck
at a time. Each piece cut his teeth, tongue, until he couldn't
        chew —
but swallowed whole each blazing chunk until a fire decked
his brain, his belly, his entire frame; until it checked
his motions, thoughts, feelings, and he became its fiery slave:
passionless, ignorant, inert, a mere mute wreck

of his former self. Then a figure, a woman, gave
him water to drink and covered him with soil and saved
his soul. But when he was recovered she would not speak or
acknowledge his presence. Every night he dreamed the same
          thing,
and became ever more troubled. He told Lucifer
of the fire and rock, and Kolob and Oliblish also, for
they were wise, but they could not find the meanings
to the signals he'd seen. However, they felt the dream's core
somehow related to the fact that creation had slowed, things
were not being produced as efficiently: Eve's
marvelous lizards were growing more sluggish than ever,
despite her efforts to mix their DNA, and beings
that should have been working toward creation's increase
          were
lurking about the cosmos, playing at craft instead of sure
experimentation: they left the fields and labs to go
meditate on their own vanities, their own fears.

Lucifer came up with an idea to lure them back: show
them the mighty expanse opened up, new lands to hollow
for their use. And he took light to the edge of the Void
but he could not penetrate the darkness, and the tow
of its tide almost pulled him under, the crashing noise
nearly broke his skull, and he marveled that his voice
was lost next to its roaring. But he believed its power
could be broken, that creation's borders could push the moist
shores ever back, ever broader. So he brought five men to stir
the Void, to chart new lands; and the five sons of Kolob were
all for a revitalized creation — for newness inflating
their edges and influences. But all their shears broke,
every shovel and pick cracked as they went to grating.

And when Kolob saw them he rebuked their prating
and swearing to find a way to expand space. For he knew
that locality had been cleared for all creating
to take place, and if the more recent creatures lacked thews
capable of the older beings' energy, the new
would soon find a way of gaining and learning; and also

he knew that to widen the Void one needed his tools
which he had brought with him from out the Abyss — no
thing made from its very own matter would shake the close
atoms, but only a hammer from refined material
would be pure enough to split the Void's stones. So
Kolob called his sons home, and told them their trial
at the Void would remain fruitless and that they had real
labors to attend to. And as they returned to their places
they reviled Kolob the more, griping for more fields
wherewith to bring forth a firmer, more powerful species.

Lucifer heard Kolob and his sons' murmur, but his searches
convinced him that to expand space was the best way to reboot
creation. He thought it wise to plumb the vast reaches
alone and not advertise his idea of opening out
area.
            Nevertheless, Kolob became worried about
the striking lack of force in newer individuals
that nagged him more consistently, and worse were the doubts
and fears expressed by those creating: a liminal
sense shadowed their purpose: if creations weren't able
to create anew, what would they do? what is the point
living? would even the Gods be endurable
to existing without focus or by dint
of their purpose originally conceived?
                              Shan't
we continue, my children and friends, he called to them when
they were assembled in the Garden Temple to recount
their ideas and troubles, It is not needful we send
explorers over the Void — we've space enough on hand
for all the work of creation. We need now to regroup
our initial enthusiasm, unify our position, and
this will be the strength that carries us, a coup
from the inside that revitalizes all.
                              Yet the troop,
despite Kolob's pleading, still followed Shinehah's words:
My brothers and sisters, to accelerate we should supe
up our lands first, then extend our borders — new land and work
have erstwhile opened the jaws of creativity, worse

means can be found, of course, but we know what to do,
and we request Kolob again break matter for the horse
and plough of creation; this is what we together choose.

Yet not all agreed with Shinehah or Kolob, and other views
were presented, until Oliblish stood and suggested,
Instead of searching for increased area and new truths
at the perimeter, let's look at what might be secreted
in the center: the Abyss. For we came invested
from out that primordial water endowed to make—
perhaps there's some secret knowledge there divested
for the willing, the able, the spade, and the rake.

Kolob trembled: No, Oliblish to journey in that lake
would be annihilation—we barely made it through, and
to reenter would be to lose creation, and that mistake,
that one be lost is one I can't endorse; it repeals the plan
of creation itself—the coldness of the Abyss rends
life, even light is useless in its darkness.
                                                    But Jehovah
stood: Kolob, I think Oliblish is wise, her council stands
firm: where else shall we go for truth? I recommend a
party be sent down through, and I invite volunteers, but
they must know of the anguish and rack inside that pit,
of the sheer force and energy required to cut
one's way out, and in, I imagine; I will get through it,
but who will come with me? And in a panic
the hosts of the cosmos erupted in debate: he shouldn't
go, he's too important to creation—but who else will fit
that role? who else the might? We wouldn't
make it, was the consensus, we aren't confident
we'd survive the Abyss.
                                        Then Lucifer quieted
the masses: I will accompany him, it is provident
I go with him—for I have light, and we will tread
the icy waters with his pith and my vision; we will shed
mystery, we will divine knowledge. But the debate lasted
long into the night, until the vote was counted
and Kolob allowed Jehovah and Lucifer precipitate

into the Abyss.
                    At dawn they stood at the cusp of fate,
their reflections looking up at them from the icy
edge of the water. They gave a bow to the senate
of the galaxy, gathered to wish them farewell and see
their daring. And they jumped, together, into the sea
of the Abyss. As they swam lower their flesh broke,
their frozen skins cracked, the chill ate them, the gravity
crushed them as they strove down.
                                    But Lucifer spoke
nothing of his fear until the pain was too much, his stroke
defeated by his grief, and he swam upward toward space,
defeated and afraid. Yet his skeletal hand wouldn't hold
the brink of the Abyss, his leg couldn't find a place
to hump the horizon. But Elkenah and Shinehah faced
him and pulled him out, their own hands rotting where
they touched the water dripping off him. Although saved
he was disgraced, and wept as Oliblish and Senshu cared
for him; as Jahoheh nursed him, Lucifer cowered, scarred
by the waters and immense pressures of the Abyss.

                                                      From
his condition Kolob and the others could only figure
Jehovah had dissolved — Lucifer remained dumb
about the misadventure, not willing to speak one
word for the fate of Jehovah, not wanting to believe
what he felt at the breaking of his own person
could happen to Jehovah. For many years he received
aid at Jahoheh's and Shinehah's hands: they nursed and relieved
his pains, but despite their arts Lucifer remained wounded,
and stayed, when he could, at his books to study
creation and energy's dissemination. Grounded,
his chores were owned by others until his health rebounded;
Jehovah's responsibilities were also divided.
In all this time creation continued, the cosmos founded
space for all in their expanding cities, and all was lighted
with a somber glow for the sorrow at losing the dead
Jehovah, the emaciated
                                    Lucifer:

                                    who remembered
Adam's tree that created worthless seed and decided
he'd plant that tree in himself: and at his word
that night he slinked into the garden, to the old cornered
area where it breathed, and he plucked a fibrous fruit,
and tried to swallow it whole, but its splintered
threads stuck in his mouth and wormed down his throat
and up in his nose until it branched and rooted, its shoots
blossom a white rose in his brain, at the base
of the skull the tree flowered again, its roots
coursing through his veins, his nerves the gossamer lace
of the tree's branches and leaves. But his face
shone as it never had, and power erupted from his
eyes—he was healed, radiated, he felt the strength waste
away his old mind and set free his old weaknesses.

And he resolved not to tell anyone of this,
but to collect Kolob's five sons, and keep them
united in a pact: for he knew that creation's limits
had to be broken at the boundary, the very hem
of space must be enlarged.

                              He called them together again,
in greatest secret for he withheld light and air
from their meeting, and they swore allegiance to him
and his plans, and he promised them the first share
of the expanded space. And they met often where
light and air would not reveal them, where no one
would touch them, and they promised to deliver
all from the loss of imagination, all creation
would once again be restored to its full operation.

Plato, I've said enough for this lyrical preface. You'll read
in *Astronomy* the effects of this negotiation,
as I've alluded in the song. For now I will leave
you to study how Pythagoras developed every deed
of the story from the stars and physics—he understood
from observation and intuition the shiny bead

universe and its history; and here is the fourth book
in the pyramid of his teaching, the final nook
before the apex: *Harmony*, how all the chapters
mesh and hold together — every particle from fire to flood,
from air to earth corresponds and dances together
in Cosmos: the harmony of eternal spheres. The Master
will guide us thus, his spirit winding up the final rapture —

At your service, with regards to your groggy instructor,

PHILOLAUS

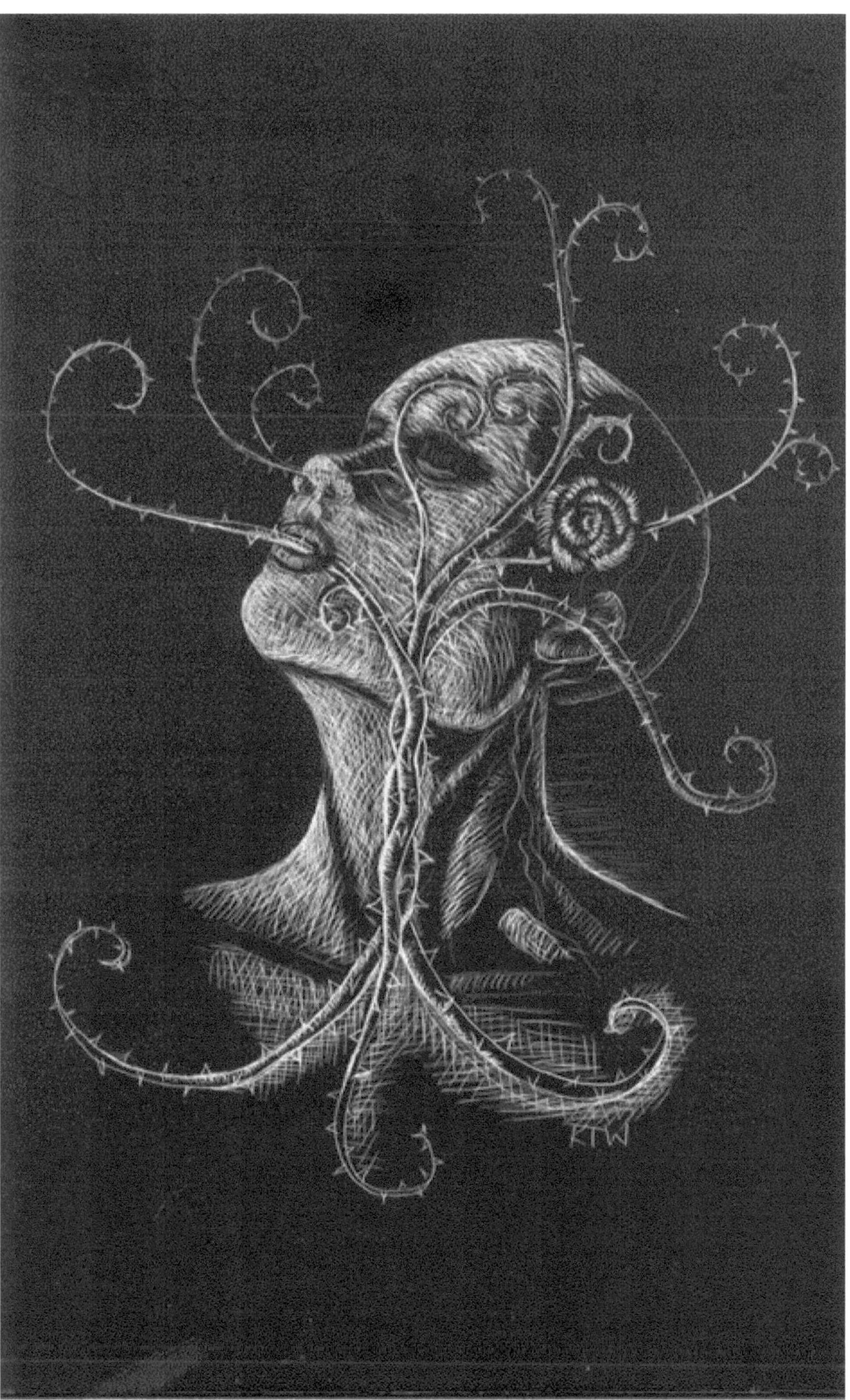

5
Apex

All the field lay quiet
       stillness followed every pant
Fallen Tumin on every hand
       flies gorging on their black eyes
To his ankles the crepitate dead foamed
       bodies cracked and rolled to his cay
But here again the old thought
       burdens short dropped in battle:
Where put the captives freed?
       How nourish these Aieswihti?
New children to his family
       a gain as sand added to sand
          Uncountable boles of uniqueness
            the pieces of water are oceans

He had advanced to the gates
       to the limits of Inturnala:
Dark city of hate and chaos
       floods of pain and whips of tears
He broke the walls and fire machines
       against the shadow army he bore his spear
He it was who trampled the horde
       electrons flashing from his mouth
Yet Lezazel evaded him
       the ruler of envy kept on the lam
As mosquitos pry at strength
       the raids of misrule nettled his hope
         Still unlost he remained on the plain
           the reaper brings in the fair harvest

Such is his report sung to the Cosmos No
          victory   Father   but respite
The enemy felled or retreated
          as pine before the saw as glaciers in thaw it is fallen
Inturnala Dark City is toppled
          black scarves twined my heart and strong arms
As Harab came menacing in hidden blades
          these I burst with a concentrated hand
Dolphin wriggle of laser   split his knives
          he lies among the slain Tumin
Their scaled bodies litter Ashaz field
          their teeth broken on the lance of my eyes
                    Their eyes shot out as I raised my war cry
                              so I have dealt with Lezazel's wraith

Next Kotan   mage dressed in likeness of power
          in the folds of lily petals she advanced
With a spell of ashy coarctation she bound me
          black boas fettered and coerced me
Down on my knees I was bound
          a rock to the mountain   a minister to misrule
And her Tumin gathered round
          tigers whose tails bite as scorpions
Kotan raised her voice in triumph
          at last the puma is bayed
But I covered them in my robe as a net
          a white circular blaze in the depths of a cave
                    And they suffocated in their tackle
                              Kotan gashed   retreated to Yaltesh
                              greatest   stygian thrall

Alone did we three meet in arms
          the shadow eclipsed as we strode on Ashaz
I was blinded by a noxious mist chalk thick
          in cimmerian reins the Aieswihti
Yaltesh commanded surround and blitzkrieg and eat
          legion stylus oxidized my flesh
Their vacant eyes groped acid through my might
          spermatozoa igniting the germ egg

And drawing inside I perceived their candor
       the clover blossoms in sun or rain
Animals trained and possessed of some talent
       turned from their will they grazed
          Life from my veins
             Unknowing under Yaltesh's bleak hex

Thus I wielded Hensholar   its spark pierced
       lightning roaring in a chasm
And I slashed all the hackamore
       the annealed filaments dwindled in flame
The Aieswihti paused their attack
       one flicker their feed released
And Kotan I struck through the left shoulder
       orca roving the sea
Yaltesh I have cleft asunder
       wolverine ravaging the mountain side
So I have dealt with the servants of Lezazel
       yet weakened he only escaped
          So now I shall rest for a season
             I'll return with the Aieswihti who might

These I will provide for as mine own
       the eagles cover the young in the nest
I have addressed the Aieswihti together
       counseled them as I have been
Hear me   you once encroached by the serpent
       intelligences wound by shades
I free you from his chains   his manacles
       his yokes   shattered as shells
For your release I strove with those chieftains
       Lezazel's camp and his hosts have I driven
Nevertheless you need not follow me   I restore
       your immortal powers   follow me if you desire
          I will grant you place among my children
             Yet you are alone to wander the aeons

Thus have I followed the path   Father
          as a learner traces his letters
Please accept these my labors
          in the garden of your palace
Lay I my bounty before thee
          the minuscule bud on the orange tree
May yet bring forth sweetness   may yet
          bring forth fruit meet for guests
So he closed his epistle to the Cosmos
          to those that meld aeon to aeon   space to space
And at dawn a mighty shout was raised
          swan wings beating as the flock rises
                    An hosanna across Ashaz   the lion's roar
                         makes even the grey stones tremble

          Glory Glory Glory

          Praise Him
          who saved us who
          showed us the folly
          of our habits

          Praise Him
          we will follow
          if we may we see
          your deeds and honor

          Amen Amen Amen

Not every Aieswihti joined him
          they took their own counsel and course
Winds pushing out on unknowable roads
          they left all others alone and in groups
He received those who willed to go with him
          and led them to his home
Yet far off his queen saw his banner
          she called the children   prepared his return
And they sang before him his tale
          of the Tumin squashed to acres of dust

Of his glory and battle they danced
       how he dashed Harab's devices   smote
         Kotan's deceitful wiles   Yaltash's bowels
           flitted to haze by his powers

After the days of jubilee were ended he
       retired to himself   to study he retreated
To focus on his burden   for where shall Aieswihti
      shed their dreamy wings and concentrate
Their energy into being   into power   into eternity
      my own land they have inhabited
And it is fruitless   trampled by wars
      and worn out with aeons   and aeons still
Are needed for its revival   too long
      have I waited to drive out the evil
And rebuild the world   She entered
      to share his brooding she twined him
        In her hair of a silken evening
          and the queen saw his burdens

Stretched desolate and sorrowful as the waste
      she commended   Your depths are known to me
You are right to sorrow for the age
      of these who choose us and their abilities
I shall meditate and counsel
      you to find out this matter for only
You can create this   such is your anointing
      such mountains are given you to raise
A dream of fulmination struck down before him
      an inkling glimpsed him that
His thought didn't need his thought
      but the subtle words of the queen
        And he knew the queen's power as she
          did not, and she untied her flowing hair

Years passed and the mountain gained strength
          the flowers broke their ash veils
For the period of rest when the animals came
          again to their fields and trails
And meditating   hunting down the cosmos
          of his heart and mind he discovered
In his soul's cortex a cell deep
          as tombs with clear waters gushing silent
It rings and rings through his mind and being
          all his eyes have found it   he sniffed out
All its borders and its continual babbling silence
          is where all his ears are turned   his hands
                    Went numb in the coldness but his
                              mouth cannot find out its name

Still it's   three years before he can force
          his eye into that cell's infinite blankness
And three years more before he can come
          back and forth as he pleases
And three more years before he turns
          to the assembled Aieswihti the children
To ask for their aid and the first
          who will venture to space
Minute as a pin point dreary and full   crushing and exotic
          where bitterness perhaps would reach through
One's fingers all fear of death and not returning
          who will be born in a world uncreated
                    Who will join the ranks of work
                              who will forsake me

6

Kapilavatthu, Sakka, Northwestern India, ~534 B. C. E.

I don't care if it's early, bring me Channa,
    for I have dreamt of ripe lotuses
    above the water, and Gotama is not found
    in his bed—so wake Suddhodana, wake

All the lanterns, all the bells, for love,
    oh, my love, what is this vision that the sight
    of you has not replaced it?

It was in a quivering bulb of light,
    and for aeons I was carried
    there, where the Gods live,
    roamed the streets and alleys
    of their magnificent palaces set with jade,
    their flowing hair tied up in silk strings.

Beyond this palace, beyond even our town in magnificence,
    or all of Sakka or Magadha, beyond the mountain
    castles and peaks was their city; their cells ranged
    one above another in sculpted cathedrals of gold.

Their traffic thick with beasts and machines
    blazing silver threads, and from trees hung pearls
    of fruits, and in every square lush gardens, life
    and vegetation dripping from every window.

And a strange invisible dust lighted
    on everything, and every burden
    doubled by this dust, by some long memory

of loss. But among the gods I spied Mara
whispering to others, and they met speaking, but only
one word could I catch, Cundra, and mushrooms fell
from their open mouths as so many words
I could neither understand nor hear until my eyes
flushed with mushrooms, and Rahula cried,
and I woke drowsy and next

Dreamt of the City of Light, everything swirling
and streaming again and Mara's band
vanished as he waved his hand, but now
I could see and hear them as other Gods could
not — their meeting and oath to create more
space, more vitality and light and beauty:

A gardener had met with Mara sometimes, unconvinced
of his gains, but their congress was open,
and Mara had much success in gleaning
brothers to his den. And they crafted a code

Immoveable to focus and force their aims
through space, as a midwife coaxes birth
they sought to give life to their conceits —

Channa — I see you are dressed
already in your driving clothes? — Listen
to this dream I've dreamt, and tell what it means:
I think only you keep the confirming signs:

Mara, wounded in a great battle, was nursed
by a woman iridescent as the moon, the rainbow
colors lit her fingers and arms. For years she nursed
him whole until he left her house and grouped the city
by talent, by calling, by force and linked them,
tried a yoke to get their motion synchronized
and effective. But all his talents wasted
away, and all his ideas sagged undernourished
and unrefining. And it seemed that in all
his bustle a dust kept settling on the city, on the Gods,
on the lands and animals.

And Mara kept his secret caucus, and their ideas were
        developed in absence,
        under the lock of night their counsel met.

The Rainbow Woman's husband, white flames consuming
        his sleeves and face, his hands shot white
        heat, whips of fire leapt from his tongue,
        caroused with Mara, kept their force
        organized. And the Rainbow Queen,
        curious of his secret, of where he vanished
        and was withheld,

Followed him out of the city;
        for three years he walked and she behind
        stayed wary of his sight, and lurked
        until in a strange avenue others emerged, his four
        brothers, and each brother five others
        and each of those five more until, off
        the road they formed an avocado
        shaped ring and vanished as they stood
        in the dense corner of some forgotten arbor.

Astonished, she waited four more years, hidden
        when at last they emerged, silent,
        and went their separate ways. And Mara
        was the last to leave and she approached him
        asking why their secret devices?

Mara refused to answer her, that only his
        enlightened circle was privy to this caliber
        knowledge, and that she would not find
        meanings even if he laid out all the signs
        and fixtures of their devotion—but salvation
        was the aim, and she should not fear,
        for he and his claque would reify creation.

She was not dissuaded, and said
        if he did not give, her husband's mind
        could be lured open. At that Mara clapped

for thunder and warned her not to interfere —
their plans only set in motion could again
gain vigor in the heavens.

She touched him on the shoulders, with her indigo
        fingers she traced his wings and wondered
        why he was so fearful, why one not an Avatar
        should take himself such responsibility? chain
        himself to phantoms of worry?

And laughed at his failed trials, at his planning
        and organization of space and creation;
        how his schemes bowed and fell through without
        even the glitter of hoarfrosted underbrush.
        With patience she admonished courage —
        for she nursed him through his fear
        of old, and said that fear resided still: Let go
        your wisdom and courage, let out the fumes
        of despair and desire, for this burden grows
        dark and its gnarled roots die
        rotten in the malformed soul —
        Why like possum scurry from garbage
        to garbage seeking what gives
        neither nourishment nor pleasure?
        And why not allow the Brahmin sit
        with your counsel? or all creation
        for you admit you work for salvation —
        let the Brahmin speak with you in your doings,
        he has led us since the beginning and is full
        powerful and wise —

But he threw her hands away, pale blanks
        he drew out their hues and grew himself
        a glistering white, his feathers mounting
        one another and peaking above the garden
        groves until she knelt beneath his haze,
        and he recounted his powers, his aids
        of war and marshaled troops ready
        and working to restore the nation:

millions of war elephants, millions of archers
set at his will, ready for his command,
the sages and magi banked and waiting
for the new stage of creation, the regeneration
of powers and forces multiplying eternally —

Without which space would rip its seams and fall
to doom and death. What could the Brahmin, locked
in his ways, without a stitch of potency? No, the old
masters had grown nearsighted and sorry, eager
ending disputations by grinding on their ruts.
But he would not let space go. For this he should be
labeled unwise? His foresight and planning had
grappled the wedges of existence together, for this
he should be satisfied with coward? No one
else had taken the pains of construction,
No one else had spent devotion weaving
creation to keep it winding through aeons
of space, and without him everything
would melt away to death — It was his
organization that made it
invisible to those who didn't heed him,
his counsel, his powers ingressing
the city, the lands, all space —

Should he then be forced to give out his talents,
his secrets when he had sacrificed his energy
for their freedom? Damn the Brahmin, he
screeched, who enslaves us to his antiquated
reins! Leave us to our work and rest
knowing one cadre won't fail regardless
the price! And in a dimple of light
he vanished, and she trembled until her color
again extended over her, and she returned home.

And in each a secret worm burrowed deep
in their hearts and continued, until in her
it lodged and her right index finger went
bulbous with white scars, and in him light

calmly left his wings, his feathers quite
dry curled at the edges even while the city
strengthened in people and palaces, even
while some omnipresent roar
wafted down on the Gods, on their machinations.

I woke with Gotama gone, Channa, and your dress
     speaks a tale sorrowful, it seems, to bear —
     but say, what can this my dream mean,
     and where is my husband that the chariot
     hastened away under the millions of stars
     beyond the guarded gate?

     Oh, Princess Yasodharâ, I beg you but see
the stables, walk once out beyond the courtyard
to the grooming stalls, and see Kanthaka dead,
and all the meanings will hold you as a mongoose
holds a cobra.

7

Fragments from
The Second Confession of Judas

Introduced and translated by Jerome T. Hirkner

The dating of this somewhat odd Gnostic text remains problematic, as does its claim to be the second of a series which has yet to be recovered. If we follow archaeological evidence, the twenty-one fragments that make up *The Second Confession of Judas* would have been composed in the late years of the second century. Indeed, the finding of these fragments among other scraps of a similar date near Naj' Hammâdî would seem to point in this direction. However, claims that this tractate is part of the mysterious thirteenth codex of the *Nag Hammadi Codices*, remnants of which were also found tucked into the cover of the sixth volume, remain spurious at best.

The date proposed above can be either supported or challenged by examining thematic parallels in other Gnostic works. In this tractate the familiar type of the Archons' rape of Zoe/Eve-of-Life, or attempted rape, are found in *On the Origin of the World*, *The Hypostasis of the Archons*, and *The Apocryphon of John*. Because of the strong thematic links with these other texts, a late second century dating is supported: its characters and themes would have been well-known and accessible to other Gnostic scribes, and perhaps even charlatans or early opponents of Gnosticism.

On the other hand, in *Judas* it is Yaldobaoth himself who performs the rape, as well as the unique and curious dismemberment of the pointedly nameless Zoe/Eve figure. And what are we to make of Luna, who doesn't seem to materialize in any other Gnostic work? Such differences lead some scholars to speculate that *Judas,* with its itemized disarticulation, predates the

Apocryphon by perhaps four centuries. Indeed, some specialists go so far as to note that such detail may illuminate early burial and embalming practices of pre-Christian Gnostics, and any biblical parallels were added by more recent, Christian scribes. The Egyptian and mythological aspects of the fragments also lend to an earlier dating, as does the fact that Irenaeus never mentions *Judas* in his *Heresies* despite its grotesque imagery—either he was unaware of the text altogether, or it had been consumed through other, later works.

In any case, due to its either much earlier or much later dating, it seems fairly safe to assume that the Judas of the title is not the same as the historic betrayer of Jesus of Nazareth.

Ultimately, in its overall importance, *Judas* reinforces the fabulous reinterpretations of scripture and myth the Gnostics engaged in and lends support to one of the central Gnostic doctrines regarding the character of Yaldobaoth.

In this translation the reclaimed fragments are numbered by the translator in an attempt to follow a linear plot; I have also preserved the text's original line length. The title is taken from the second half of the first fragment's first sentence; the first half of that sentence is lost.

Fragments from
The Second Confession of Judas

(1) [It was in the] waiting that Yaldobaoth remembered
her finger sprinkling a vital [luminescence]
along his wings and shoulders, the touch
and beauty of her light (? Sophia) [form fractured

(2) Rainbows which] bend but never break through
schemes, never generate true power despite [. . .]
radiance; and as Yaldobaoth longed for [might he felt] it
in his heart to take her shimmering image; overcome,
control [and defilement] was his aim:

(3) First to merge [his image] with hers and take
every ounce of light (? Sophia) and force, then break
[her image] entire, shatter every light shard
in the grinding axle of the cosmos.

(4) [At her door] he thought [this], and her children
left, and her husband was away, so he slipped
inside the door and chained [it, *fem. sing.*] deftly.

(5) And [in the kitchen, without language]
he attacked her, as she stooped to trim the basil
he lunged and devoured her [clothing in ashes] gripping
her lips in [his] teeth, her thighs chaffed by the slink
of dry feathers, her belly abraded as by pine
needles; the oily claw bit through the paper petals.

(6) So [Luna] was brought forth by her
left side; and [Luna's] face turns always
away, always cold as abysmal waters
she seeks the tough border of light
(? Sophia) where the end of peace and power await.

(7) When Yaldabaoth saw [Luna] spring [from her
side], the hideous form [. . .] of his notions,
he gouged out her eyes, with his talons he seethed
through her gooseberry eyes;

(8) [Clamping his] mouth on her nose he sucked
out her brains in fine [yarns or strings];

(9) And strangled her with his lopping tongue
wrapped as [wires or twine] her throat was
the wet, nutating linguiform member;

(10) Her ears [he snapped off] with his fingers,
her lips he swallowed whole, two slugs
limply greasing the sides of his mouth
[. . .] as she stopped breathing.

(11) He hacked her arms with a dull flint knife,
and her legs and hip joints taking [also at the shoulder, the arm]
each finger and toe to bury each all over
space: in gardens and lots, in [refuse mounds]
where nobody looks, in the thick lands
and swamps, in the hearts of mountains.

(12) He ate her clear hair and it crunched like sand;
with his nails he razed her skin to filaments;
her bowels he lobbed heavy on the sizzling fire.

(13) The bones he also clacked onto flame, save
the skull and pelvis he fastened with ribs
and wires [twine] for the [? Mitre of Death] to perform
all the rites of his order;

(14) Violet finger and toenails he scattered
[with bats] racing out over lakes at dusk, [and mice]
lost them [at his] bidding in their nests and hoards.

(15) But he boiled [the spine], in fire
he disfigured the bones and hardened
their edges, then wrapped them in red
[lettuce leafs] and brought them to Adam:

(16) This material here, can a wedge [? ploughshare]
be fashioned of it? For [it, *masc. sing.*] may split
the void and aid creation — it has some light (? Sophia)
still soaking in its core.

(17) And Adam [*neg.*, did not] know the bones
for never had he handled such or seen,
and he wondered at Yaldobaoth's ore;

(18) I have synthesized this of elements
panned at the brink of the abyss, squelched
from [*pos.*, my] tattered garments have I rescued this bit
of matter, and tampered the particles to mass —
but can you form it to a tool? For you [alone]
possess the necessary equipment. Keep
me this your promise, and I'll make
sure of your reward and power — think
of the [ageless] space [ready for] our new aeons.

(19) So Adam swore an oath to Yaldobaoth to make
it from her bones, yet he knew it
not; and she [Eve also] aided him, but to no avail;
and for years they were foiled [in their work and] kept
their calling secret from the others [gods], even
from every other [Archon], such was their oath.

(20) And all this time a great mourning went up for [her]:
for no one knew whence [Luna] came: some said [she; *lit:*
her] was punished [. . .] transformed to [Luna], while others
said [Luna] devoured her [. . .] [a daemon] to torment
them in their loss [of generative force].

(21) And creation continued slowly, and [Luna] stayed
[in the] kitchen, without language where
she was born [. . .] without saying or hearing or seeing
anyone, touching but the floor and always facing
the corner, the northwest [corner]
is where she sat [herself] alone and constant
to an urge to escape or perish, scratching
her right shoulder, her neck.

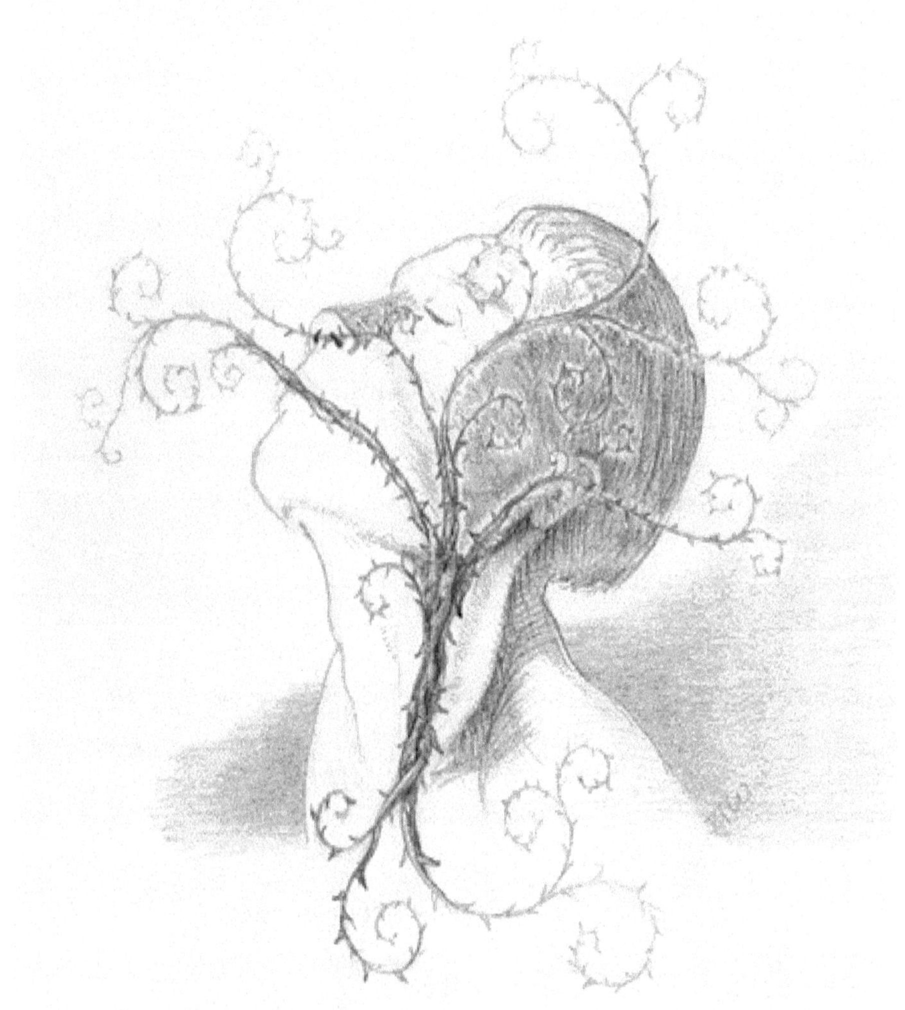

8

Pyramid of the Sun, Teotihuacan, Mexico, ~385

H'men! We are in our last dress:
black and red for the wisdom that shall turn
from this people — the third band of priests
taking our sacramental knowledge. To the North —
this temple face points our direction, and our faces
go beyond Tula, beyond thorns and deserts,
beyond the ice where the Ahua alone rules
us henceforth.
                    The chief has chosen Tonatecuhtli,
so-called deity of plenty, and the Sun for this
place and people, and we,
brothers, will cart our divinations from the very veins
of this teopan temple to escape
defilement.
                              This is our lot,
                                        here — scratch

out, burn, bust up and carry small pieces
only, destroy the carvings
and paintings all along this northern relief before
the sun, yet, any second now,
after Quetzalcoatl rises: The beginning

  edge:
                    Here is Hueteotl
                                  vexed at creation,
    the mighty city all
                        around him,
              the shivering creations

huddled   upabove one
                                                          another
though he continues with his coa to plant seed
in the universe with Challicue they both continue. And
Xochpilli, inventor and carer, here
                                        absorbed with working
                                                out the coa for
                        Mictlan, also known as Vucub, Prince
of Deceit. But you see this
                                tells how Xochpilli
                                        fails always
        creating   thattool,   always his attempts
fumbled.
                        And Mictaln's xibalba grows in darkness
binding their arms along
        each other the serpentine oath of life
or death in their conference.
                                Vucub sees the power
absent in Xochpilli is knowledge and here hurries
Xochpilli to taste of the ceibu tree —
                                this jade wrought
                        of the trunk, here, formed
myself and consecrated even
                        before you were born,
                        young priests —
finding Mayahuel in the green
                                house he says weakness
                wrenches every talent
                        corroded snail
        shell, easily fatigued
                                and broken —
Listen, sweet Mayahuel,
every power will reside
        along your shoulders, strike
forth from every finger for this fruit gave me
                                        strength for
my   near miss   inthe abysmal
                                        well   left
        me strainedanddepleted until

                         its   chalky fibers
netted my mouth   raw
sinews congealing — take this, eat yourself
to know
              Despite Quetzcoatl's caution
              and the tree's sterility he gave
                    her half a ceibu seed
                            indigo, her white hairs
                            flow over her
                            arms akimbo, upand
                    swallow flitting through her
                                 lips
                                               which
routed down it spiny tendrils   her throat
                                       full chocked
rot   nota   gurgle but midnight
                                                    rose
                   gushing her mind, a spike
punctured her breast and bore a pumpkin in her womb,
countless dangling seeds around the basin
                                        of her womb —
                        After one day
Vucub roused
                her, gave herone the
other half seed to share and called
Xochpilli   eat
          gain the glory of your mate; Mayahuel,
                            this key
                            mystery, all the gates
                            of talent
                                   bashed
                            by you, complete
                            the task creation —
You'll awaken whole worlds

                              beautiful, makeable, full
of women chasing butterflies,
                         of long-feathered birds
          gracing down and healing the children

                their silver spells spilling down the fiery beaks

this was his speech, like a bat
                                his feathers rubberized
in lone long stretch of evening, all the eagles

                                                        swooped
out the garden, one skin cape
                                    drappedown Vucub's arms
                        Xochpilli ate and was seized
through the nose,
                    clusters of blossoms
                        breaking his brain bowl—
            see his face go
forward here, his skull sprouting vines
                                theroots weaving
                                    out through the ends
                        thetuberseminate
                        his groins and his eyes
opened
the next evening near Mayahuel
        when Mictlan had gone
his arms heavy
with strength, a puma
lunging wildly at the babe so
                            he renewed his task
the flame
                at the forge
blazing   he cooled his goal
                        in the waters brought from the Abyss
                            and called   Mayahuel
        to see his work,
                        the Ixcoa
                        inlaid
                        obsidian
                        forthe
                        blade,
                        bone
                        handle

                              with
                              jade/
                              life jac-
                              ulate
                              every
                              point
                    And she was amazed at this, formerly
               it never held shape, it denied all their forces

and they called on
          Mictlan   streakedinlikelightning
                    bolts and he was
          triumphant,
                    promised   aeons but
Xochpilli and Mayahuel would not
          accept his offers   they saw
                                        their powers
                                        rising greater
                              the morning sun disfigures
                    every star and   Mictlan

quakedand fled
and vowed revenge
for their opulence   against
his silky wings   He gathered his sons,
          of Hueteotl first,   now gnarled
                    as Vucub's crown
                    of death:
                    Camozotz
          Zipacua   Piltintec
Cauac

                    Cabraca

                              — Piltintec being chief
                              though youngest over
                              the heavenly element and
                              fierce in glory, leader
                              of vultures, aboder
                              of grubs   These
Mictlan gathered and stopped Hueteotl in his field —
                                                  Here

Hueteotl, we are endowed with might,
                                        grant you thehonor
                              as is   custom to break
the Void
          again
                                  for it is your place and station
                  and you must give the first
                        lot   to Piltzintec whose wife is lost
who was instrumental in obtaining Ixcoa
                        to sow the seed
                                of creation into burgeoning
fields once again,
          and saving again our station   But see
how Vucub's teeth
                              are bent
                              around his silver lies, mother
                              of pearl brought
                              from the great eastern waters
                                    Hueteotl saw
Mictlan's glory and marveled, for none
was endowed save he
                        to break tools
                              granting space and creation
but Mictlan would never speak
                              his powers, admit
                              the cavernous appetite hurtling
                  through his bowels to own creation
                  himself and halt
                  Hueteotl
          withthe   juices
          cruising inhim left by the tiny white worms
burrowing deep inside
                        for fear
consumed
the dark Vucub, and he knew   not to break space
and rooted on Hueteotl —
                                    You must use Ixcoa
                        first, for you are the first, see

                              your sons all
rise up to behold you
                         Under the tradition
guise ofallthewrong fates   Hueteotl made
his way with Challicue,
                                                   to the end
and edge of the Void   a jaguar roaming
                         out upon the plain
                         roaring deep
                         amidst the sleeping
                         women, babies
                         nipped in cradle
                         deep, and no moon dark
                              followed
by Mictlan's xibalba
          the five sons and their five
                    princes and their five princes
                    beyond all these while
the high apartments
darkened, heaven's Teopan
fires blown out
                         by Mictlan's claws   flapping
Here they are, scratch
in below thestone, crackout
                                   every shell
                    of jade, every painted
                              figure out
                    the plaster   Now
                         they stand around
                              wait
to see   the Void   tamed
                    and expanded
          curlicue motif
          embedded pearls,
          gold laid and paint
          violet, orange,
                    these swathes of blue
                         from the clouds, all the mountains

                    lowered equal all
                    these oceans plain
                                    tranquil
from bustle and clangor
            in the weakened creations   to
                                        pasture and palaces
                            fit and ready for
                        their unique impression
                        ability and talents molding
                and chiseling with power and speed
                    every age a renaissance
            without the decay   oftheir
                                                living
time

And Hueteotl took Ixcoa
                        beneath
                                Mictlan's
dove-   hopeful eye,
and drove the blade
into the asphalt   buried

And here
                the sun has popped
                the eastern peak
while all the light
is bursting golden   Quetzcoatl sputters
from the Abyss
                        dripping sparks
                        flinging when he blinks
        at   the   center   of Cosmos

explosionsent

                every

                                star

                                                falling.

9
The Fifth Blessing from Mount Peor

¶   And when he looked on the moon
rising above the still blue sky he took up
his parable, and said, Pick up your ears
all the Earth, every face turn forward in
alarum —

      My tongue flaps to tatters
in God's levanter, his heavy cord
wizens my bellows;

      On my lips he placed his holy mint
leaf, my throat he plays as the psalmist's
harp strings;

      Crystalline waters gush
from his mouth into mine, pure snow
melt of divinity floods my low plain:

      Hearken ye kings of the Canaanite
nations, for Jehovah rose argent through
the heavens, and every electron echoed
the voice from the gleaming Monad:
This second time Jehovah
conquers, and pleases Me.

      Hear then, lords of every station,
from he whose eye is awake though
opened, who speaks one stitch the wound
that rent creation is bound by, his miracle:

¶   Though the universe cracked
and washed away as fine dust in clear
mountain streams,

        In one hundred twenty three shards, squares
and triangles, heaven's palatium cracked, space
fled in every direction,

        And Jehovah yet wastes
no energy, quick to the sea run
spring waters; for Kolob, ashamed
at his weakness was loth to return
with Oliblish to their workstead.

        But Jehovah took them
together, and set them nearest again
the Abyss, just beyond its dark horizon;
and Kolob delivered the satchel to Jehovah
and tethered the cosmos setting
forth all the motions into proportions
with Oliblish; love pulled all the cords into
order, anchored in loose matter, as reins
combed in their strong fingers were the cosmos
roped. Kolob and Oliblish drove time
from thence, forth from the vigorous
well of the center.

¶   Though Kolob's sons dissipated, chaff
swept off by the zephyr, Jehovah
sped to them, in their agony falling,

        In five phosphorescent bearings
these petal blossoms streaked, trionum
hibiscus or hand fully agape,
the very hand of God opening, one hole
centered organizes everything;
he sped to them

      And snatched them in their shame,
linked them and their scattered mates for each
restoring each: for Elkeneh, Rukeneh
waits, Senshu pleads before Karesh, Mintrah sings
along Libnah's weary face, for Mahmacknah
Sepdet serves a feast;

      At Sepdet's feast Mahmacknah prays, Libnah
solemn plays sitar for Mintrah, Karesh
speaks comfort for Senshu, Rukeneh brings
dusty Elkeneh from the door;

      Daughters and sons spin on Kolob's spokes, motion
gearing up toward motion, each lifting
each and holding.

¶   Yet volcanic Shinehah was left alone,
every star and atom of debris fled
past his scorching touch.

      And Jehovah called forth Earth,
the name bound up in Jahoheh;

      Straightway every flick and ounce
crept to him ignoring all the holocaust, shells
and remnants reuniting, and there
Jehovah assembled Earth, stacked
mitochondria sequoia, each sea wave
of hair placed in degree;

      His flaming breath brought her life
renewed, the lava flow of his word
sealed again her soul

      Who recalled existence and rushed
to lost Shinehah, and danced in a magnesium flame
before him,

While he weeps at her dancing, at any
small distance.

When Olea felt her mother
return she fled to her, yet keeps
her face hidden from her mother, tinkling
pirouettes she seeks the deep
places of her father between
Shinehah and her mother.

¶   Thus he called forth all creation,
every quark was mated for salvation: all
the timber weighs on the next to stand
as pyramid walls, as stones in the arch limp
tightly on their brothers.

Adam and Eve came last to his eye
from the tap roots of creation crawled they;

And Jehovah asked for their strength,
an adamantine son kneels for the aged's blessing
hand:

For Ahura Mazdah is the One, Indefatigable
Whisper racing in every grain
of creation, of matter, His Hand spans
the cosmic cubit, His Eye seeks every low
corner;

His Command is as the tremor,
who shall stand before the wrenching
universe?

The ocean's sucked up in His Glance, forests
flee before His Word; yet stillness keep
the mountains, firm the granite rocks
stay until He Calls them;

       And we are yet too poor
for power. I've one great challenge yet
to make then raise the banners, trump
degeneration's scamp through Ahura Mazdah's
veins;

       For I emerged in his hoary Mind,
and wrestled the marshaled legions there,
and flew into His mouth, His eye
held me all the while, and there He spoke
my name out loud and there I leapt
from His auric lips and His attendants
burried me in smoldering tobacco
leaves to shield me from His holy graze.

       And there He taught me all
His ways, and here I've orchestrated
creation — but one remains.

¶   Thus the covenant was born
for creation and joy, some harmony spilt
glistening through the aeons.

       And hear, oh kings of all the nations,
for yet he is building his armies,
his generals mark red their maps;

       Close now he comes to Lucifer,
on the beak of the Void's retreat
into space, and close he will fold
his brother into courage, into love:

       And his people will not be mistaken;
his work will uphold the heavens, the people
know whose arm is awakened: the third number
accomplishes the sure salvation, the fourth secures
millennial bliss, and the last files us in
his graces:

This is his blessing out
upon his children through the cosmos;
this is the might linked atom to atom,
tent rows arranged in genealogy.

¶   And when Balak heard this
he smote Balaam with his rod, and he said
unto Balaam, This fifth time you were
to curse mine enemies and
yet you bless them.

Do not the Moabite gods speak
in clearer forms? have we not priests
enough to wrangle out divinities?

Why speak you this Unknown Word?

What need have we of your strange
beasts? does the Peacock know
the Lion?

And he smote him again
and departed with his retinue.

And Balaam convulsed
on the stony ground, blood bubbles
snapped from his fractured tongue.

אש
רוח
8
6
9
7
5
3
4
1
עפר
2
מים
שו

www.ingramcontent.com/pod-product-compliance
Lightning Source LLC
LaVergne TN
LVHW051503170726
843492LV00002B/790